ODES
John Keats

ODES
John Keats

 Spruce Alley Press

2016

Odes by John Keats

First Printing: 2016
ISBN 978-1-329-79674-4
Spruce Alley Press   www.sprucealley.com

Odes by John Keats is a new edition derived from these public domain source texts: LAMIA, ISABELLA, THE EVE OF ST. AGNES, and OTHER POEMS, London: Taylor and Hessey, Fleet-Street, 1820; John Keats, POETICAL WORKS, 1884 (at Bartleby.com); The Oxford Book of English Verse, 1919 (Bartleby.com); and KEATS' POETICAL WORKS, ed. H. Buxton Forman, 1908.

Contents

Introduction

When John Keats perished from tuberculosis at age 25 in a small rented room in Rome, he didn't think he had written anything that would survive the ages. He had left England lonely, short of money, his hopes of success crushed, pained with the knowledge that he had no time to change his circumstances. Of the three books published during his lifetime, none sold well, and contemporaneous reviews were generally dismissive, even contemptuous. Aside from a small circle of London friends and artists, Keats, so it seemed, would become but an afterthought in English literary history. Convinced of this fate, he asked that his gravestone be marked with the epitaph: "Here lies one who's name is writ in water." The poems in this volume would change all that.

Keats' "great odes" were included in his third and final book (1820), but little notice was taken of them until after his death. They were written in a burst of creative energy in the Spring of 1819. We do not know the order of composition, aside from a few clues. The "Bards of Passion" ode (usually not included among the great odes, though it appeared in the same volume) was written in early 1819, and it can be seen as a forerunner of the others. In the Spring of that year, "Ode to Psyche" came first. It marked a breakthrough in Keats' lyrical style, and the poet was obviously driven to write more in that vein. The other odes quickly followed suit (in what order, we are not sure, except for "To Autumn" which is supposed to have been the last).

This edition collects all the poems in Keats' oeuvre that have been titled as Odes, including the odes published in Keats' 1820 book LAMIA, ISABELLA, The EVE OF ST. AGNES and OTHER POEMS. Also included are the posthumous and fugitive poems "Ode to Apollo," "Ode to Fanny," "Ode on Indolence," and "Fragment of an Ode to Maia." The sequencing of the poems is my editorial choice, not Keats'. Indeed, the poems can be read in any order or in isolation.

Biographer Walter Jackson Bate tells how, near the end of his life, Keats bitterly refused to read letters and claimed to be "through with books." But in the final weeks, something changed. He asked his friend Joseph Severn to read to him. Soon, the resentment was gone. As Bate retells it, "Keats kept calling for more and more books to be near him.... He was of course unable to read. But hour after hour, for three full days, the mere presence of these books acted on him (to use Severn's word) as a 'charm.'"

The poems Keats left us are charms themselves—enchanting, lofty, deep, ambiguous. This is the kind of book to keep close at hand. To keep you company. To keep coming back to. To remind you that in the face of life's mystery, you are not alone.

- James Esch

Ode to Apollo

In thy western halls of gold
   When thou sittest in thy state,
Bards, that erst sublimely told
   Heroic deeds, and sang of fate,
With fervour seize their adamantine lyres,
Whose chords are solid rays, and twinkle radiant fires.

Here Homer with his nervous arms
   Strikes the twanging harp of war,
And even the western splendour warms,
   While the trumpets sound afar:
But, what creates the most intense surprise,
His soul looks out through renovated eyes.

Then, through thy Temple wide, melodious swells
   The sweet majestic tone of Maro's lyre:
The soul delighted on each accent dwells,—
   Enraptur'd dwells,—not daring to respire,
The while he tells of grief around a funeral pyre.

'Tis awful silence then again;
   Expectant stand the spheres;
   Breathless the laurell'd peers,
Nor move, till ends the lofty strain,
Nor move till Milton's tuneful thunders cease,
And leave once more the ravish'd heavens in peace.

Thou biddest Shakspeare wave his hand,
   And quickly forward spring
The Passions—a terrific band—
   And each vibrates the string
That with its tyrant temper best accords,
While from their Master's lips pour forth the inspiring words.

A silver trumpet Spenser blows,
    And, as its martial notes to silence flee,
From a virgin chorus flows
    A hymn in praise of spotless Chastity.
'Tis still! Wild warblings from the Æolian lyre
Enchantment softly breathe, and tremblingly expire.

Next thy Tasso's ardent numbers
    Float along the pleased air,
Calling youth from idle slumbers,
    Rousing them from Pleasure's lair:—
Then o'er the strings his fingers gently move,
And melt the soul to pity and to love.

But when Thou joinest with the Nine,
And all the powers of song combine,
    We listen here on earth:
Thy dying tones that fill the air,
And charm the ear of evening fair,
From thee, great God of Bards, receive their heavenly birth.

Ode to Fanny

I

PHYSICIAN Nature! Let my spririt blood!
   O ease my heart of verse and let me rest;
Throw me upon thy Tripod, till the flood
   Of stifling numbers ebbs from my full breast.
A theme! a theme! great nature! give a theme;
     Let me begin my dream.
I come—I see thee, as thou standest there,
Beckon me not into the wintry air.

II

Ah! dearest love, sweet home of all my fears,
   And hopes, and joys, and panting miseries,—
Tonight, if I may guess, thy beauty wears
     A smile of such delight,
     As brillinat and as bright,
As when with ravished, aching, vassal eyes,
     Lost in soft amaze,
     I gaze, I gaze!

III

Who now, with greedy looks, eats up my feast?
   What stare outfaces now my silver moon!
Ah! keep that hand unravished at the least;
     Let, let, the amorous burn—
     But pr'ythee, do not turn
The current of your heart from me so soon.
     O! save, in charity,
     The quickest pulse for me.

IV

Save it for me, sweet love! though music breathe
   Voluptuous visions into the warm air;
Though swimming through the dance's dangerous wreath,
      Be like an April day,
      Smiling and cold and gay,
A temperate lilly, temperate as fair;
      Then, Heaven! there will be
      A warmer June for me.

V

Why, this, you'll say, my Fanny! is not true:
   Put your soft hand upon your snowy side,
Where the heart beats: confess—'tis nowthing new—
      Must not a woman be
      A feather on the sea,
Sway'd to and fro by every wind and tide?
      Of as uncertain speed
      As blow-ball from the mead?

VI

I know it—and to know it is despair
   To one who loves you as I love, sweet Fanny!
Whose heart goes fluttering for you every where,
      Nor, when away you roam,
      Dare keep its wretched home,
  Love, love alone, his pains severe and many:
      Then, loveliest! keep me free,
      From torturing jealousy.

VII

Ah! if you prize my subdued soul above
   The poor, the fading, brief, pride of an hour;
Let none profane my Holy See of love,
      Or with a rude hand break
      The sacramental cake:
Let none else touch the just new-budded flower;
      If not—may my eyes close,
      Love! on their lost repose.

Fragment of an Ode to Maia

written on May Day, 1818

Mother of Hermes! and still youthful Maia!
    May I sing to thee
As thou was hymned on the shores of Baiæ?
    Or may I woo thee
In earlier Sicilan? or thy smiles
Seek as they once were sought, in Grecian isles,
By Bards who died content on pleasant sward,
Leaving great verse unto a little clan?
O give me their old vigour, and unheard,
  Save of the quiet Primrose, and the span
    Of Heaven and few ears
Rounded by thee, my song should die away
    Content as theirs,
Rich in the simple worship of a day.—

Ode on Indolence

They toil not, neither do they spin.

I

One morn before me were three figures seen,
With bowed necks, and joined hands, side-faced;
And one behind the other stepp'd serene,
In placid sandals, and in white robes graced;
They pass'd, like figures on a marble urn
When shifted round to see the other side;
They came again, as, when the urn once more
Is shifted round, the first seen shades return;
And they were strange to me, as may betide
With vases, to one deep in Phidian lore.

II

How is it, Shadows! that I knew ye not?
How came ye muffled in so hush a masque?
Was it a silent deep-disguised plot
To steal away, and leave without a task
My idle days? Ripe was the drowsy hour;
The blissful cloud of summer-indolence
Benumb'd my eyes; my pulse grew less and less;
Pain had no sting, and pleasure's wreath no flower:
O, why did ye not melt, and leave my sense
Unhaunted quite of all but-nothingness?

III

A third time pass'd they by, and passing, turn'd
Each one the face a moment whiles to me;
Then faded, and to follow them I burn'd
And ach'd for wings because I knew the three;

The first was a fair Maid, and Love her name;
The second was Ambition, pale of Cheek,
And ever watchful with fatigued eye;
The last, whom I love more, the more of blame
Is heap'd upon her, maiden most unmeek,—
I knew to be my demon Poesy.

IV

They faded, and, forsooth! I wanted wings:
O folly! What is love! and where is it?
And for that poor Ambition! it springs
From a man's little heart's short fever-fit;
For Poesy! - no, - she has not a joy,—
At least for me, - so sweet as drowsy noons,
And evenings steep'd in honied indolence;
O, for an age so shelter'd from annoy,
That I may never know how change the moons,
Or hear the voice of busy common-sense!

V

And once more came they by;—alas! wherefore?
My sleep had been embroider'd with dim dreams;
My soul had been a lawn besprinkled o'er
With flowers, and stirring shades, and baffled beams:
The morn was clouded, but no shower fell,
Tho' in her lids hung the sweet tears of May;
The open casement press'd a new-leav'd vine,
Let in the budding warmth and throstle's lay;
O Shadows! 'twas a time to bid farewell!
Upon your skirts had fallen no tears of mine.

VI

So, ye three Ghosts, adieu! Ye cannot raise
My head cool-bedded in the flowery grass;
For I would not be dieted with praise,
A pet-lamb in a sentimental farce!
Fade softly from my eyes, and be once more
In masque-like figures on the dreamy urn;
Farewell! I yet have visions for the night,
And for the day faint visions there is store;
Vanish, ye Phantoms! from my idle spright,
Into the clouds, and never more return!

ODE
("BARDS OF PASSION AND OF MIRTH")

Bards of Passion and of Mirth,
Ye have left your souls on earth!
Have ye souls in heaven too,
Double-lived in regions new?
Yes, and those of heaven commune
With the spheres of sun and moon;
With the noise of fountains wond'rous,
And the parle of voices thund'rous;
With the whisper of heaven's trees
And one another, in soft ease
Seated on Elysian lawns
Brows'd by none but Dian's fawns;
Underneath large blue-bells tented,
Where the daisies are rose-scented,
And the rose herself has got
Perfume which on earth is not;
Where the nightingale doth sing
Not a senseless, tranced thing,
But divine melodious truth;
Philosophic numbers smooth;
Tales and golden histories
Of heaven and its mysteries.

Thus ye live on high, and then
On the earth ye live again;
And the souls ye left behind you
Teach us, here, the way to find you,
Where your other souls are joying,
Never slumber'd, never cloying.
Here, your earth-born souls still speak
To mortals, of their little week;
Of their sorrows and delights;
Of their passions and their spites;
Of their glory and their shame;
What doth strengthen and what maim.
Thus ye teach us, every day,
Wisdom, though fled far away.

Bards of Passion and of Mirth,
Ye have left your souls on earth!
Ye have souls in heaven too,
Double-lived in regions new!

Ode to Psyche

O Goddess! hear these tuneless numbers, wrung
  By sweet enforcement and remembrance dear,
And pardon that thy secrets should be sung
  Even into thine own soft-conched ear:
Surely I dreamt to-day, or did I see
  The winged Psyche with awaken'd eyes?
I wander'd in a forest thoughtlessly,
  And, on the sudden, fainting with surprise,
Saw two fair creatures, couched side by side
  In deepest grass, beneath the whisp'ring roof
  Of leaves and trembled blossoms, where there ran
        A brooklet, scarce espied:

'Mid hush'd, cool-rooted flowers, fragrant-eyed,
  Blue, silver-white, and budded Tyrian,
They lay calm-breathing on the bedded grass;
  Their arms embraced, and their pinions too;
  Their lips touch'd not, but had not bade adieu,
As if disjoined by soft-handed slumber,
And ready still past kisses to outnumber
  At tender eye-dawn of aurorean love:
        The winged boy I knew;
But who wast thou, O happy, happy dove?
        His Psyche true!

O latest born and loveliest vision far
  Of all Olympus' faded hierarchy!
Fairer than Phoebe's sapphire-region'd star,

Or Vesper, amorous glow-worm of the sky;
Fairer than these, though temple thou hast none,
      Nor altar heap'd with flowers;
Nor virgin-choir to make delicious moan
      Upon the midnight hours;
No voice, no lute, no pipe, no incense sweet
  From chain-swung censer teeming;
No shrine, no grove, no oracle, no heat
  Of pale-mouth'd prophet dreaming.

O brightest! though too late for antique vows,
  Too, too late for the fond believing lyre,
When holy were the haunted forest boughs,
  Holy the air, the water, and the fire;
Yet even in these days so far retir'd
  From happy pieties, thy lucent fans,
  Fluttering among the faint Olympians,
I see, and sing, by my own eyes inspir'd.
So let me be thy choir, and make a moan
      Upon the midnight hours;
Thy voice, thy lute, thy pipe, thy incense sweet
  From swinged censer teeming;
Thy shrine, thy grove, thy oracle, thy heat
  Of pale-mouth'd prophet dreaming.

Yes, I will be thy priest, and build a fane
  In some untrodden region of my mind,
Where branched thoughts, new grown with pleasant pain,

Instead of pines shall murmur in the wind:
Far, far around shall those dark-cluster'd trees
  Fledge the wild-ridged mountains steep by steep;
And there by zephyrs, streams, and birds, and bees,
  The moss-lain Dryads shall be lull'd to sleep;
And in the midst of this wide quietness
A rosy sanctuary will I dress
With the wreath'd trellis of a working brain,
  With buds, and bells, and stars without a name,
With all the gardener Fancy e'er could feign,
  Who breeding flowers, will never breed the same:
And there shall be for thee all soft delight
  That shadowy thought can win,
A bright torch, and a casement ope at night,
  To let the warm Love in!

Ode on a Grecian Urn

I

Thou still unravish'd bride of quietness,
  Thou foster-child of silence and slow time,
Sylvan historian, who canst thus express
  A flowery tale more sweetly than our rhyme:
What leaf-fring'd legend haunts about thy shape
  Of deities or mortals, or of both,
    In Tempe or the dales of Arcady?
  What men or gods are these? What maidens loth?
  What mad pursuit? What struggle to escape?
    What pipes and timbrels? What wild ecstasy?

II

Heard melodies are sweet, but those unheard
  Are sweeter; therefore, ye soft pipes, play on;
Not to the sensual ear, but, more endear'd,
  Pipe to the spirit ditties of no tone:
Fair youth, beneath the trees, thou canst not leave
  Thy song, nor ever can those trees be bare;
    Bold Lover, never, never canst thou kiss,
Though winning near the goal—yet, do not grieve;
  She cannot fade, though thou hast not thy bliss,
    For ever wilt thou love, and she be fair!

III

Ah, happy, happy boughs! that cannot shed
  Your leaves, nor ever bid the Spring adieu;
And, happy melodist, unwearied,
  For ever piping songs for ever new;
More happy love! more happy, happy love!
  For ever warm and still to be enjoy'd,

For ever panting, and for ever young;
All breathing human passion far above,
  That leaves a heart high-sorrowful and cloy'd,
  A burning forehead, and a parching tongue.

IV

Who are these coming to the sacrifice?
  To what green altar, O mysterious priest,
Lead'st thou that heifer lowing at the skies,
  And all her silken flanks with garlands drest?
What little town by river or sea shore,
  Or mountain-built with peaceful citadel,
  Is emptied of this folk, this pious morn?
And, little town, thy streets for evermore
  Will silent be; and not a soul to tell
  Why thou art desolate, can e'er return.

V

O Attic shape! Fair attitude! with brede
  Of marble men and maidens overwrought,
With forest branches and the trodden weed;
  Thou, silent form, dost tease us out of thought
As doth eternity: Cold Pastoral!
  When old age shall this generation waste,
  Thou shalt remain, in midst of other woe
Than ours, a friend to man, to whom thou say'st,
  "Beauty is truth, truth beauty,"—that is all
  Ye know on earth, and all ye need to know.

Ode to a Nightingale

I

My heart aches, and a drowsy numbness pains
  My sense, as though of hemlock I had drunk,
Or emptied some dull opiate to the drains
  One minute past, and Lethe-wards had sunk:
'Tis not through envy of thy happy lot,
  But being too happy in thine happiness,—
    That thou, light-winged Dryad of the trees,
        In some melodious plot
  Of beechen green, and shadows numberless,
    Singest of summer in full-throated ease.

II

O, for a draught of vintage! that hath been
  Cool'd a long age in the deep-delved earth,
Tasting of Flora and the country green,
  Dance, and Provencal song, and sunburnt mirth!
O for a beaker full of the warm South,
  Full of the true, the blushful Hippocrene,
    With beaded bubbles winking at the brim,
        And purple-stained mouth;
  That I might drink, and leave the world unseen,
    And with thee fade away into the forest dim:

III

Fade far away, dissolve, and quite forget
  What thou among the leaves hast never known,
The weariness, the fever, and the fret
  Here, where men sit and hear each other groan;
Where palsy shakes a few, sad, last gray hairs,
  Where youth grows pale, and spectre-thin, and dies;

Where but to think is to be full of sorrow
    And leaden-eyed despairs,
Where Beauty cannot keep her lustrous eyes,
    Or new Love pine at them beyond tomorrow.

IV

Away! away! for I will fly to thee,
  Not charioted by Bacchus and his pards,
But on the viewless wings of Poesy,
  Though the dull brain perplexes and retards:
Already with thee! tender is the night,
  And haply the Queen-Moon is on her throne,
    Cluster'd around by all her starry Fays;
      But here there is no light,
  Save what from heaven is with the breezes blown
    Through verdurous glooms and winding mossy ways.

V

I cannot see what flowers are at my feet,
  Nor what soft incense hangs upon the boughs,
But, in embalmed darkness, guess each sweet
  Wherewith the seasonable month endows
The grass, the thicket, and the fruit-tree wild;
  White hawthorn, and the pastoral eglantine;
    Fast fading violets cover'd up in leaves;
      And mid-May's eldest child,
  The coming musk-rose, full of dewy wine,
    The murmurous haunt of flies on summer eves.

VI

Darkling I listen; and, for many a time
  I have been half in love with easeful Death,
Call'd him soft names in many a mused rhyme,
  To take into the air my quiet breath;

Now more than ever seems it rich to die,
  To cease upon the midnight with no pain,
    While thou art pouring forth thy soul abroad
        In such an ecstasy!
  Still wouldst thou sing, and I have ears in vain—
    To thy high requiem become a sod.

VII

Thou wast not born for death, immortal Bird!
  No hungry generations tread thee down;
The voice I hear this passing night was heard
  In ancient days by emperor and clown:
Perhaps the self-same song that found a path
  Through the sad heart of Ruth, when, sick for home,
    She stood in tears amid the alien corn;
        The same that oft-times hath
  Charm'd magic casements, opening on the foam
  Of perilous seas, in faery lands forlorn.

VIII

Forlorn! the very word is like a bell
  To toil me back from thee to my sole self!
Adieu! the fancy cannot cheat so well
  As she is fam'd to do, deceiving elf.
Adieu! adieu! thy plaintive anthem fades
  Past the near meadows, over the still stream,
    Up the hill-side; and now 'tis buried deep
        In the next valley-glades:
  Was it a vision, or a waking dream?
    Fled is that music:—Do I wake or sleep?

Ode on Melancholy

I

No, no, go not to Lethe, neither twist
Wolf's-bane, tight-rooted, for its poisonous wine;
Nor suffer thy pale forehead to be kiss'd
By nightshade, ruby grape of Proserpine;
Make not your rosary of yew-berries,
Nor let the beetle, nor the death-moth be
Your mournful Psyche, nor the downy owl
A partner in your sorrow's mysteries;
For shade to shade will come too drowsily,
And drown the wakeful anguish of the soul.

II

But when the melancholy fit shall fall
Sudden from heaven like a weeping cloud,
That fosters the droop-headed flowers all,
And hides the green hill in an April shroud;
Then glut thy sorrow on a morning rose,
Or on the rainbow of the salt sand-wave,
Or on the wealth of globed peonies;
Or if thy mistress some rich anger shows,
Emprison her soft hand, and let her rave,
And feed deep, deep upon her peerless eyes.

III

She dwells with Beauty—Beauty that must die;
And Joy, whose hand is ever at his lips
Bidding adieu; and aching Pleasure nigh,
Turning to Poison while the bee-mouth sips:
Ay, in the very temple of delight
Veil'd Melancholy has her sovran shrine,
Though seen of none save him whose strenuous tongue
Can burst Joy's grape against his palate fine;
His soul shall taste the sadness of her might,
And be among her cloudy trophies hung.

To Autumn

I

Season of mists and mellow fruitfulness,
  Close bosom-friend of the maturing sun;
Conspiring with him how to load and bless
  With fruit the vines that round the thatch-eves run;
To bend with apples the moss'd cottage-trees,
  And fill all fruit with ripeness to the core;
        To swell the gourd, and plump the hazel shells
  With a sweet kernel; to set budding more,
And still more, later flowers for the bees,
Until they think warm days will never cease,
        For Summer has o'er-brimm'd their clammy cells.

II

Who hath not seen thee oft amid thy store?
  Sometimes whoever seeks abroad may find
Thee sitting careless on a granary floor,
  Thy hair soft-lifted by the winnowing wind;
Or on a half-reap'd furrow sound asleep,
  Drows'd with the fume of poppies, while thy hook
        Spares the next swath and all its twined flowers:
And sometimes like a gleaner thou dost keep
  Steady thy laden head across a brook;
  Or by a cyder-press, with patient look,
        Thou watchest the last oozings hours by hours.

III

Where are the songs of Spring? Ay, where are they?
  Think not of them, thou hast thy music too,—
While barred clouds bloom the soft-dying day,
  And touch the stubble plains with rosy hue;
Then in a wailful choir the small gnats mourn
  Among the river sallows, borne aloft
        Or sinking as the light wind lives or dies;
And full-grown lambs loud bleat from hilly bourn;
  Hedge-crickets sing; and now with treble soft
  The red-breast whistles from a garden-croft;
        And gathering swallows twitter in the skies.